The day is quiet.

The air is still. No breeze blows.

The leaves on the trees do not move. Blades of grass do not move. Even the birds are still and quiet.

The afternoon air is hot, so hot that it is hard to breathe. People wipe their faces. "The air is hot," they say, "hot and sticky."

There are big clouds in the sky. They are bright white.
The air near the earth pushes hot air up and through each
high cloud.

The air goes up fast and spills over at the top of the clouds.
The clouds get bigger and bigger. The tops of the clouds
reach higher and higher.
You can see the clouds grow bigger and darker as you watch
them.

Pilots of airplanes stay out of these clouds.

The air rushing upward might carry the airplane with it.

The air might turn the plane upside down or break it apart.

4

The clouds grow still bigger and bigger. They tower higher
and higher.
One of these clouds may be ten miles from bottom to top.
The cloud gets thicker and thicker. The cloud gets blacker
and blacker.
People say, "There's going to be a storm. You can tell
because it's hot and there are black clouds in the sky."

The air carries water to the clouds. The water is a gas. It is
water vapor. The water vapor changes to water droplets.
Each little droplet carries ions.
An ion is a tiny charged particle, a bit of electricity.
Each little droplet carries a tiny bit of electricity. We say
each droplet has a small electric charge.

10

There are billions and billions of droplets in a cloud.

There are billions and billions of electric charges in a cloud.

The whole cloud is charged with electricity.

When the charge is very big, electricity jumps from the top of the cloud to the bottom.

This makes a flash of lightning.

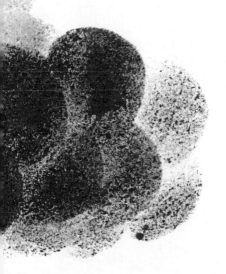

The skies get darker.

A sprinkle of rain makes dark spots on the sidewalk.

The wind blows hard.

The rain falls faster and harder. It blows against the windows and doors.

Water races down the street.

The lightning continues to flash.

It may flash from the top of a cloud to the bottom.

Lightning may flash from one cloud to another.

It may flash from a cloud to a high building or to a tree.

The flash of lightning is followed by thunder.
Thunder may be a rumble or a roar.
It may be a loud, crackling crash.
Sometimes thunder sounds like an explosion.

When there is lightning, air is heated. The hot air around
the lightning is pushed out. It is pushed out faster than
sound travels. The sound waves catch up with one
another. That's why there's so much noise.

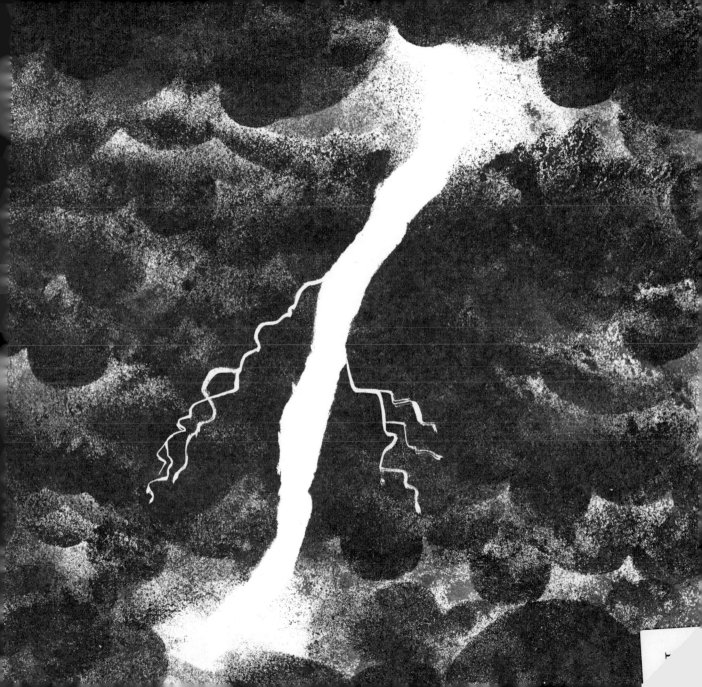

Sound travels through the air. It travels quite slowly.
Some airplanes travel faster than the sound that they make.
They are supersonic planes.
When planes go faster than the sound they make, the planes
break the sound barrier. You hear a loud, booming crack.

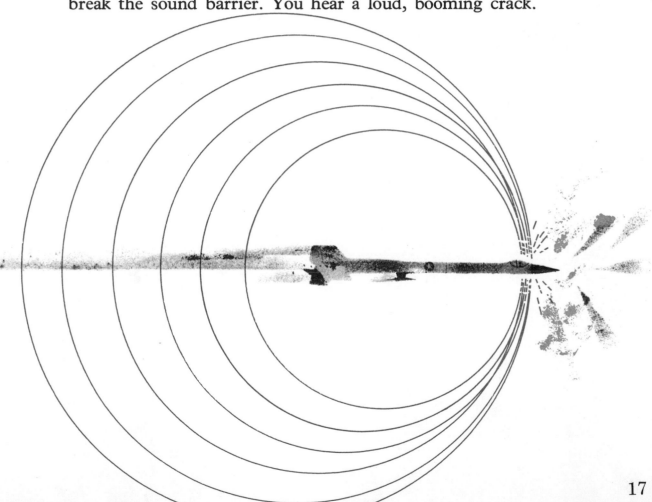

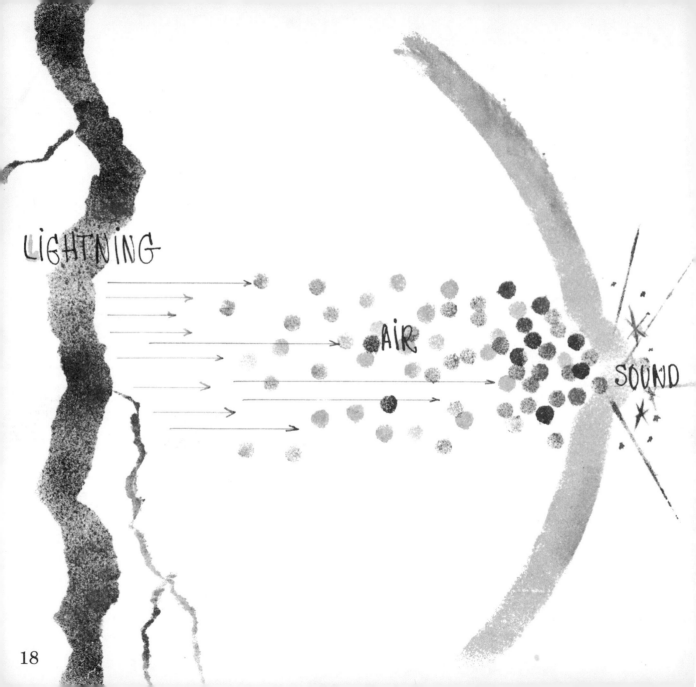

LIGHTNING

AIR

SOUND

18

When there is thunder, air is pushed aside faster than the
  sound travels.
The air catches up with the sound that was made earlier,
  and you hear a loud, crashing boom.
When the thunder is far away, the sound rumbles and rolls.

Lightning pushes air, air crashes into sound.

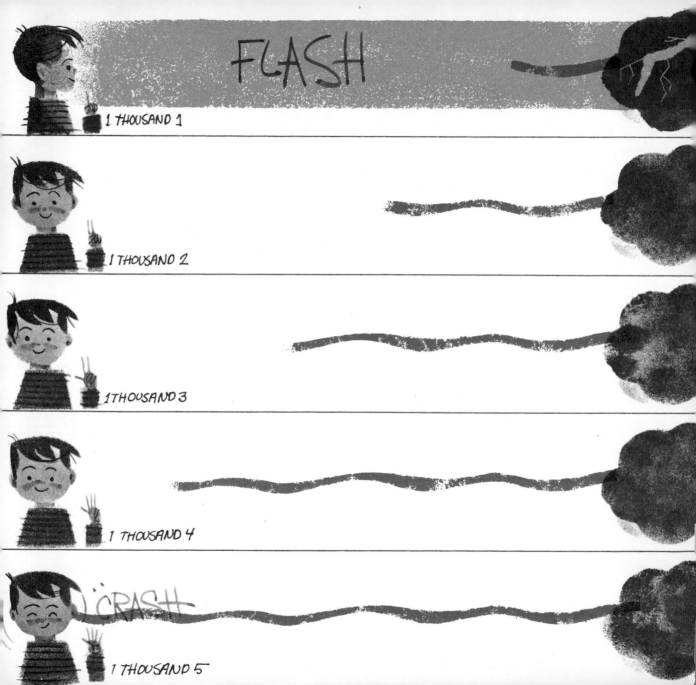

You see lightning the moment it flashes because light travels very fast.

Sound travels much more slowly than light.

It takes about five seconds for sound to travel one mile.

Here is a way you can count five seconds. Watch the second hand of a clock while you say these words: "One thousand one, one thousand two, one thousand three, one thousand four, one thousand five."

See if you can say them in just five seconds. You may have to count a little faster or a little more slowly.

When you see a flash of lightning, count the seconds this way until you hear the sound of thunder.

If five seconds go by, the storm is one mile away.

If ten seconds go by, the storm is about two miles away.

Sometimes we have thunder storms in winter.
But most storms with big flashes of lightning and loud
   roaring thunder happen late in the afternoon on a summer
   day.

Some dogs try to hide when they hear thunder.
Most people don't like the noise either.
But thunder does not hurt anyone.

Lightning is different.

Lightning may start fires in houses or barns.

It may start forest fires.

Lightning may knock over trees and telephone poles.

It may kill cows and horses in a field. It may kill people, too.
Most people are killed because they don't know what to do
to protect themselves.
Lightning is nothing to be afraid of if you do the right thing.

If you are in swimming, get out.

If you are outside, go inside.

When a storm is close, stay away from the stove, the telephone, and the windows.

When a storm is close, stay away from the bathtub and the shower.

This is one time when it's all right not to wash.

If you are in a car during a lightning storm, stay there.
That is just about the safest place there is.

If you are caught outdoors, don't stand under a tall tree that is alone in a field.

Lightning usually strikes the highest thing there is.

It might strike the tree.

If you are in a big field, get down as low as you can.

Don't stand up and be the highest thing around.

Keep away from metal fences or metal pipes stuck in the ground because they may carry electricity.

The next time you see dark clouds on a still, hot summer afternoon, watch them from a safe place.
The clouds may grow and become a storm.
Then lightning flashes, thunder rumbles, the wind blows, and rain falls in a downpour.

People used to think that lightning was the fiery fingers of an angry god. They thought that he made thunder when he rumbled and roared.
They feared the storms as they feared their gods.

But there is no reason for you to fear storms.
You know what makes the thunder and lightning.
You know what to do to keep safe.

About the Author

Franklyn M. Branley is Chairman and Astronomer at the American Museum— Hayden Planetarium. The author of more than fifty books, for many years he has helped children learn scientific facts and principles, building and expanding their sense of wonder about the world they live in. Dr. Branley has taught science at many levels, including the elementary grades, high school, college, and graduate school. With Dr. Roma Gans, he supervises and edits the Let's-Read-and-Find-Out series.

Dr. Branley studied at the State University of New York College at New Paltz, at New York University, and Columbia University. He lives with his wife in Woodcliff Lake, New Jersey. They have two daughters.

About the Illustrator

When he is not writing or illustrating, Ed Emberley pursues several interesting hobbies. He prints limited editions of children's books on his own hand press, studies Early Americana, and experiments with toy-making.

Mr. Emberley received a Bachelor of Fine Arts degree from the Massachusetts College of Art in Boston. He lives in Ipswich, Massachusetts, with his family.